PEKING OPERA FACIAL DESIGNS

京剧脸谱

FOREIGN LANGUAGES PRESS BEIJING

外文出版社　北京

PEKING OPERA FACIAL DESIGNS

The "painted faces" (*hualian*) or the *jing* characters in traditional Chinese operas may have originated as masks or the designs painted on their faces by primitive people at sacrificial and divination rituals. Whatever its origin, the "painted face" tradition can be traced back into the mists of time. In their long process of evolution, different types of opera gradually developed stylized patterns for their characters. These stylized patterns are commonly called "face charts" (*lianpu*).

Based on the styles of the local operas in Hubei and Anhui provinces, Peking Opera has also drawn from the operas of Shanxi and Shaanxi provinces for its facial patterns. As a result of the efforts made by *jing* artists of several generations, the facial patterns of *jing* characters numbering over 100 ——have gradually developed their own peculiarities, and turned into an important part of the art of Peking Opera.

By and large, the facial patterns of Peking Opera have the following characteristics:

First, beautiful and varied patterns. In drawing these patterns, the makeup artists divide the face into three parts, centering around the brows, eyes and bridge of the nose, respectively. This is called a "three-tile" face. The variations in color and pattern reflect the different characteristics and temperaments of the different roles.

Second, flamboyant and symbolic colors: Colors can give expression to people's emotions of love, hate, etc. The facial paintings of Peking Opera make full use of the Chinese people's traditional aesthetic views. On the Peking Opera stage, red stands for loyalty and generosity; Guan Yu (a famous and loyal general of the State of Shu during the Three Kingdoms Period) is an outstanding example of a role in which red is extensively used. Black indicates honesty and straightforwardness, and two typical examples of roles in which black is used are those of Bao Zheng (or "Lord Bao") and Li Kui. Yellow denotes valor and dauntlessness, and is used in such roles as those of Dian Wei (a brave general under Cao Cao during the Three Kingdoms Period) and Huang Santai (a heroic outlaw of the Qing Dynasty). Blue designates boldness and fierceness, and a typical example of a role in which blue is used is that of Shan Xiongxin (a ruffian who lived from the end of the Sui Dynasty to the early stage of the Tang Dynasty). Green indicates impetuousness, and is used in the role of Ma Wu (a faithful follower of Liu Xiu, the founding emperor of the Eastern Han Dynasty). Finally, white denotes craftiness and treacherousness; white is predominant in the role of Cao Cao (the founder of the State of Wei in the Three Kingdoms Period).

Third, exquisite and rich means of expression: There are four basic methods employed when painting an opera performer's face: rubbing, delineating, smearing and breaking. Rubbing involves applying colors to the entire face with fingers, paying particular attention to the eyebrows, eyes and veins. Delineating means applying greasepaint with brushes and drawing various patterns on the face. Smearing means plastering the face white with a brush and then delineating the eyes and brows. Breaking means drawing asymmetrical patterns on the face. These four methods can be used either independently or together to enhance the artistic effects. In addition, for immortals and ghost characters, the method of touching up the face with gold and silver foil is also employed.

Fourth, a wide variety of schools. In Peking Opera, there are many different schools of *jing* characters. Jin Shaoshan, He Shouchen, Hou Xirui and Qiu Shengrong are only four of their most important representatives. While striving for their own artistic perfection, highly accomplished Peking Opera artists have all made painstaking efforts to develop their own styles of facial patterns, thus adding unique characteristics to the different schools that they represent.

As an important aspect of the entire Peking Opera art, facial patterns have, over the past more than 100 years, been enriched and become much appreciated by audiences. Moreover, various types of handicrafts have been developed on the basis of Peking Opera facial patterns and made them familiar far and wide.

京 剧 脸 谱

　　"花脸"是传统戏曲中净角独特的化妆形式。有人说它由假面具演变而成，有人说起源于古代祭祀驱邪活动，可见它历史的悠久。中国戏曲在长期演变发展中，不同的剧种、不同的人物逐渐形成了相对固定的程式化的谱式。这就是人们常说的脸谱。

　　京剧脸谱是在汉、徽等地方戏的风格上，又吸收了山、陕梆子的刻画特点。经过几代净角艺术家的创造，逐渐形成了门类丰富、流派纷呈的独特风格，成为京剧艺术的重要组成部分。

　　欣赏京剧脸谱，大体可从如下的几个特色上着眼：

　　一、　美妙多变的图案：以眉、眼、鼻窝为主把面部分为三块，称"三块瓦"脸谱，它是勾脸的基本构成，由此衍化出各种彩色的花"三块瓦"脸和图案变化丰富的碎脸，结合不同人物的特征、性格，精心刻画，变化无穷。常见的就有百种之多。

　　二、　夸张象征的色彩：色彩可以表达人的爱憎，脸谱充分利用了中国人的传统审美观念，京剧舞台上，红色表示忠义英勇，如关羽；黑色表示肃穆刚直，如包公、李逵；黄色表示勇猛彪悍，像典韦、黄三太；蓝色表示狰狞残暴，如单雄信；绿色表示粗莽憨直，如马武；白色表示奸诈诡佞，如曹操。

　　三、　细腻丰富的手法：京剧脸谱有揉、勾、抹、破四种基本描绘手法。揉脸是用手指将颜色揉满脸部，再加画眉、目及纹理。勾脸是用毛笔调油色在面部勾画各种图案。抹脸是用毛笔蘸白粉把面部涂白，再略点染眉、目。破脸指在面部勾画不对称的歪脸。几种手法既独立运用又相互组合，可造成更丰富的效果。另外，属神怪等剧中人物还有敷金、贴银的手法。

　　四、　不断创新的流派：京剧的净行流派纷呈，金少山、郝寿臣、侯喜瑞、裘盛戎只是最重要的代表。造诣精深的艺术家，追求自身艺术的完美，在脸谱的勾画上也无不独具匠心，各具风格，成为流派体系中鲜明的特色。

　　京剧脸谱作为京剧艺术整体中重要的组成部分，一百余年，不断丰富发展，被人们喜爱。各种形式的脸谱工艺品，在民间流传，更加扩大了它的艺术影响。

Characters and Role Categories in Peking Opera

The Peking Opera repertoire runs to more than 1,000 items, all of which tell and retell touching stories of sorrow, happiness, separation and reunion. Their rich and varied characters leave indelible impressions in the minds of opera audiences, and very distinct role characterizations have emerged over the years in Peking Opera, which are referred to as "role categories."

The "role categories" comprise individual sets of characteristics, including gender, age, temperament and status. In Peking Opera, the characters on stage are generally divided into four types, namely, *sheng*, *dan*, *jing* and *chou* (male, female, painted face and clown). The actors and actresses tend to specialize in one or two of these role categories.

京剧的角色与行当

数以千计的京剧剧目，不知演绎了多少悲欢离合的动人故事。丰富多彩的角色，以其鲜明的舞台形象让人难以忘怀。京剧艺术家依据各类角色的特征，在表演形式上做了明显的区分和高度的概括。这就产生了京剧的"行当"。

"行当"是中国传统戏曲中表现某些特定类型角色的专业分工。京剧艺术一般把舞台上的人物依性别、年龄、性格、身份的不同分为生、旦、净、丑四个类型。演员也以专门表演其中某一、二类角色的行当来分工。

Laosheng (Old Man): As the name suggests, actors (actresses in rare cases) in this role category perform the roles of middle-aged and older males, with light makeup and wearing finely decorated costumes. In accordance with the differences of age of the characters, they wear artificial beards or whiskers of black, gray or white.

老生：通常表演中、老年男性角色。俊扮、化淡妆。以年龄的不同分别戴黑、灰、白颜色的髯口（即假胡须）。

Xiaosheng (Young Man): Artists in this role category play young male roles (typically young scholars). They usually wear fine costumes. Over a thin layer of pinkish powder covering the whole face, greasepaint is used to delineate the eyes and brows, to suggest the vitality of youth.

小生：扮演青年男性角色。俊扮，面部略施朱粉，以油彩描绘眉目，形象光彩漂亮，显示出青春的活力。

Dan (Female): Mainly depicting middle-aged and young female roles, the actresses (actors in rare cases) usually wear heavy makeup. Their cheeks are mostly painted red to set off the powdery white of the forehead, nose and jaw. Heavy black grease-paint is used to highlight the eyes and brows, and red color is applied to the lips to demonstrate the classical beauty of Chinese women.

旦：主要表现剧中青年女性。重施朱粉，两颊红润衬出额、鼻、颌的粉白；油黑的重彩描绘美丽的眉眼，一点朱唇颜色十分鲜明。显示了中国女性的古典美。

Laodan (Old Female): The makeup is usually light, with light delineation of the corners of the eyes and cheeks to give the audience the impression that the characters have reached the evening of their lives and are reliable and steady.

老旦：扮演老年妇女，化淡妆。眼角、两颊略做描画，使人感到人物已近暮年，苍老而稳重。

Jing (Painted Face): Exaggerated colors are used to depict bold, powerful and fierce male characters. The range of these styles is the most intriguing in the whole of traditional opera.

净：扮演豪放、威武、凶猛、彪悍的男性角色。用夸张的色彩和一定的谱式在面部绘成不同的图案，即"脸谱"。是传统戏曲化妆中最具特色的方法。

Chou (Clown): These are usually nimble, witty, humorous or cunning minor characters. The face patterns are rather simple; it is only necessary to draw different shapes of white spots around the ridge of the nose and delineate the eyes and brows.

丑：通常表现那些灵巧、机敏、幽默、狡猾的小人物。其谱式较简单，只在鼻梁周围画上不同形状的白色块并略点眉目，十分生动。

I. *Zheng Lian* (Face Preparation)

"Face preparation" is the first stage of theatrical makeup. The methods of "rubbing" and "smearing" are employed to apply the basic color to the entire face. On this basic color, heavier colors are used to depict the eyes, brows, mouth and nose as well as the veins of the facial muscles. Broadly speaking, "face preparation" includes *shuibailian* (water-white face), *roulian* (rubbed face) in different colors and *taijianlian* (eunuch's face) evolved on the basis of the rubbed face.

To prepare the "water-white face," it is first necessary to smear the entire face with a white color, and then paint the eyelids and brows with black, gray or other colors. On the stage, actors with such painted faces mainly play the roles of treacherous and hypocritical officials.

For a "rubbed face," first mix different types of greasepaint in the palm and apply the mixture to the face in a thin layer. The commonly used colors are reddish brown, gray and black. The depiction of the five sense organs is relatively realistic, with just little exaggeration. the "rubbed face" is common on the stage.

一、整脸

"整脸"，是戏曲化妆的初始形式。整个面部用"揉"、"抹"两种方式涂成一种基本色彩。在底色的基础上加重描绘眉、目、口、鼻等器官和面部肌肉纹络。"整脸"一般包括"水白脸"、各色"揉脸"以及演变的"太监脸"等。

"水白脸"，用毛笔把面部涂成白色，以黑、灰等色点画眉目。舞台上多用于表现身居高位，奸诈伪善，油光粉面的反面人物。

"揉脸"，在手掌上调成不同油彩薄薄地揉涂于面部，常见有红、褐、灰、黑等色彩。五官描绘比较写实，略作夸张，舞台上适用范围较大。

9

(chart 1) (谱式1)

⑬ Cao Cao in *A Meeting of Heroes*. Cao Cao is an important character in many operas based on stories from the Three Kingdoms Period (220–280). For more about the opera, please see the related synopsis at the back of the book.

Water-white face: The brows and eyes are narrow, and the crow's claws at the corners of the eyes and wrinkles on the forehead are clearly noticeable. In the space between the eyebrows, a red dot signifies a prime minister and commander-in-chief, as well as a sinister and skeptical disposition.

《群英会》之曹操，三国戏中重要人物。（详见后页相关剧目介绍，下同。）

"水白脸"，单眉细眼，两道鱼尾纹和额头纹明显，印堂略点朱红，显示一品宰相、三军主帅气派和多疑狡诈的性格。

11

⑭ Sun Quan in *Ganlu Temple*. Sun Quan is the king of the State of Wu in operas about the Three Kingdoms Period.

Water-white face: The eyebrows are somewhat raised, the face is heavily colored and the eyes are wide open. The wrinkles between the eyebrows are closely knitted. With purple nasal sockets and mustache, the facial pattern is meant to depict the character as being both crafty and gallant.

《甘露寺》之孙权，三国戏中吴国国君。

"水白脸"，赤眉微竖，重脸瞠目，印堂纹紧锁，紫鼻窝配紫胡须，狡诈中透出威武之气。

⑮ Sima Yi in *The Empty City Ruse*. Sima Yi is a major character in some Peking Opera plots based on stories from the Three Kingdoms Period.

Water-white face: With brows shaped like wooden clubs and narrow eyes, as well as white hair and beard, this crafty and sharp-witted character also has a steady and stately air as commander-in-chief of the Wei army.

《空城计》之司马懿，三国戏中魏国主帅。

"水白脸"，棒锤眉，眯缝眼，白发皓髯，机敏奸诈中更显出稳重威武的军事统帅的神气。

12

⑯ Yan Song in *Beating Yan Song*. Yan Song was a treacherous court official of the Ming Dynasty (1368–1644).

　　Water–white face: With lightly curved brows, triangular eyes and red paint between the brows, the character has an oily face clearly crisscrossed by lines, presenting the vivid image of a high court official who has disarming looks but is extremely treacherous inwardly.

《打严嵩》之严嵩，明代（公元 1368 – 1644 年）有名的奸臣权相。

　　"水白脸"，淡弯眉、三角眼、油光面、红印堂。眉攒中纹络交错。相貌平常而内心奸诈的权奸形象。

⑰ Guan Yu in *Huarong Path*. Guan Yu was a famous general of the Kingdom of Shu in the Three Kingdoms Period.

First, the face is prepared and rubbed red, and then dark lines are applied to the brows and eyes. Long lines on the forehead and the dark nostrils depict an outstanding hero who inspires awe by upholding justice.

《华容道》之关羽，三国戏中蜀国大将。

红色整脸揉脸，用浓黑的线条勾画出卧蚕眉，丹凤眼，长长的额头纹，简略的黑鼻窝，展现出大义凛然，威武崇高的英雄形象。

14

(18) Zhao Kuangyin in *Escorting Jingniang Home*. Zhao Kuangyin was the founder of the Song Dynasty (960-1279).

The face is prepared red; the black eyebrows and white eye sockets imply a dragon, and the red color signifies a dignified and imposing nature, reflecting the canonization of this historical figure by traditional opera.

《千里送京娘》之赵匡胤，宋朝的开国皇帝。

红色整脸，黑眉白窝隐寓一条潜龙，红色显示堂堂正正。反映了传统戏曲对这一人物的肯定。

⑲ Bao Zheng in *The Scholar's Wife*.

Bao Zheng (999–1062), also known as Lord Bao, has long been considered by the Chinese people as the epitome of an upright official. Hence, his facial pattern has unique characteristics—black all over, and with slight touches of red on the cheeks. The most noticeable features are the white crescent on the forehead and white eye sockets that look like the Diagram of the Supreme Ultimate. The whole design appropriately gives expression to the unique disposition of this honest official.

《秦香莲》之包拯。

包公（公元999－1062年）是民间的铁面无私的清官的象征。包公的脸谱也独具特色，满面通黑，两颊微红。最具特色的是脑门上的白月牙和两道太极图似的白眉窝，黑白分明。恰如其分地表现了这位刚直不阿的传奇清官的特征。

15

⑳ Liu Jin in *Famen Temple*. Liu Jin was a eunuch of the Ming Dynasty (1368–1644).

This is the typical facial pattern for a eunuch, derived from the prepared face, which can be divided into areas for red, oily white and other colors. The eyebrows, eyes and mouth are slightly exaggerated to give the impression of a person who is overbearing and supercilious.

《法门寺》之刘瑾，明代的宦官。

太监脸，是由整脸演化而来的，有红色和油白色等。勾画时眉眼口略作夸张，显示骄横得意、目空一切的神气。

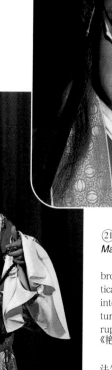

㉑ The martial arts instructor in *Sunny Mansion*.

A typical rubbed face using brown. Simple delineation of the vertical brows and the staring eyes bring into full prominence the repulsive features of a villainous lackey of a corrupt official.

《艳阳楼》之武教师。

褐色"揉脸"，竖眉瞪目，简练的手法勾画出一副恶奴走狗的嘴脸。

II. *San Kuai Wa Lian* (Three-Tile Face)

The "three-tile face" is the basic form of Peking Opera facial design. First, a brush is used to delineate the eyebrows, the eye sockets and nostrils to divide the face into three empty parts, namely, the forehead and the left and right cheeks. Then fill the empty spaces with different colors to form the designs appropriate for the character. In line with Chinese tradition, the different colors have different connotations, which can be summed up as follows: Red—loyalty and bravery; yellow—aggression and brutality; blue—dauntlessness and treachery; white—arrogance and resourcefulness; black—uprightness and awesomeness; green—intrepidness and irascibility; purple—honesty and bravery; and pink-vigor in old age.

二、三块瓦脸

"三块瓦脸"是京剧脸谱的基本勾画形式。用毛笔以黑颜色勾画出眉、眼窝和鼻窝，把面部分割为额头，左右两颊三块空白，在这三块空白中填以不同颜色即绘成不同颜色的三块瓦脸。通过人们传统审美观赋予颜色不同寓意，可以构成适用于众多角色的脸谱。各种颜色的寓意可概括为：红，忠义、英武。黄，忠勇、凶暴。兰，刚强、阴险。白，傲慢、矜持。黑，正直、威武。绿，彪悍、暴躁。紫，刚正、勇猛。粉色，鹤发童颜。

17

(chart 2) （谱式2）

18

㉒ Jiang Wei in *Tielong Mountain*. Jiang Wei was the commander of the troops of the Kingdom of Shu in the later part of the Three Kingdoms Period.

Red three-tile face: The basic color all over the face is red, with the eyebrows and eyes painted black and the area above the brows painted white, to produce an impression of solemnity and stateliness. In addition, the Diagram of the Supreme Ultimate in the middle of the forehead indicates the wisdom and resourcefulness of a great general despite the fact the state he served was beyond rescue.

《铁龙山》之姜维，三国后期蜀国军事统帅。

红三块瓦脸，黑眉眼，白眉窝配朱红色面部，庄重威严。额中一幅太极图表明这位力挽狂澜的蜀国将军的智慧与才能。

23 Chao Gai in *Three Attacks on Zhu Family Village*. Chao Gai is a leader of the outlaws of Liangshan Mountain in operas adapted from the classical novel *Outlaws of the Marsh*.

Yellow three-tile face: In the novel *Outlaws of the Marsh*, Chao Gai is depicted as a man of superhuman strength. The basic yellow color is meant to show the character's intrepidity, while the red dot between the brows signifies his fidelity and integrity.

《三打祝家庄》之晁盖，水浒戏中梁山义军头领。

黄三块瓦脸，小说中描绘晁盖曾力举千钧铁塔，黄色显示了人物的彪悍，印堂一点红心，象征他以忠义为本。

19

㉔ **Xiahou Dun in** *Changbanpo*. Xiahou Dun is a general under Cao Cao in operas based on stories of the Three Kingdoms Period.

Blue three-tile face: In *Romance of the Three Kingdoms*, Xiahou Dun is hit by an arrow in the eye. When he pulls the arrow out, the eyeball comes out with it. He then eats his own eyeball, showing how ferocious he is. The basic blue color is meant to produce in people a sense of fear.

《长坂坡》之夏侯惇，三国戏中曹操麾下战将。

蓝三块瓦脸，小说中描写他曾在战场上吃掉自己被冷箭射伤的眼球，其凶猛顽强由此可见。蓝脸使人感到阴冷可怕。

㉕ **Zhang He in** *Changbanpo*. Zhang He is also a general under Cao Cao in operas based on stories of the Three Kingdoms Period.

Purple three-tile face: According to *Romance of the Three Kingdoms*, Zhang He was bold and skillful at fighting. Moreover, he was extremely loyal to the Kingdom of Wei ruled by Cao Cao. The warped eyebrows and eyes indicate his valor, while the purple face implies loyalty.

《长坂坡》之张郃，三国戏中曹操麾下战将。

紫三块瓦脸，张郃勇猛善战，忠于曹魏，翘曲的眉眼表现了勇猛，紫色脸膛以寓其忠心。

㉖ Ma Su in *The Loss of the Strategic Jieting Pass*. Ma Su was a general of the Kingdom of Shu. In one battle with troops of the Kingdom of Wei, he was so conceited that he refused to take any advice from others. As a result, he lost a strategic pass to the enemy.

Oily white three-tile face: The succinct delineation of the eyebrows and eyes produces the impression that this character is haughty and conceited.

《失街亭》之马谡，三国戏中蜀国大将。

　一次与敌交战，不听劝告，失掉了战略要地街亭。

　油白三块瓦脸，眉眼简洁,给人以傲慢、矜持、刚愎自用的感觉。

21

㉗ Xu Sheng in *The Romance of Liu Bei and Sun Shangxiang*. Xu Sheng is a general of the Kingdom of Wu in operas based on stories of the Three Kingdoms Period.

His facial pattern, a variation of the "three-tile face," is like a shoe-shaped silver ingot. The forehead is painted red, the cheeks are painted white, and the eyebrows, eyes and nasal sockets are painted black. This facial pattern is usually used for lower-ranking military officers.

《龙凤呈祥》之徐盛，三国戏中东吴战将。

　元宝脸额头红色，面颊白色，油黑眉眼鼻窝，是三块瓦脸的衍变，此谱式一般用于中下层将官。

㉘ Zhang Dingbian in *The Jiujiang Estuary*. Zhang Dingbian was a leader of a peasant rebellion in the mid-14th century.

Pinkish white three-tile face: The undulating eyebrows and the lines extending from the corners of the eyes are meant to display the characteristics of an aging general, while the red dot between the eyebrows and the pinkish color on the cheeks are to indicate the mien of someone who is getting on in years but is still very vigorous.

《九江口》之张定边，14 世纪中叶起义军将领。

　粉白老三块瓦脸，起伏的眉眼和眼角的垂线以显示老年武将的特征，印堂红心，粉色面颊表现了人物老当益壮的神采。

III. *Hua San Kuai Wa Lian* (Three-Tile Face with Flowery Patterns)

On the basis of the "three-tile face" more meticulous and flexible methods are adopted in the treatment of the eyebrows, the eye sockets and the nostrils, to produce different designs that depict more accurately the disposition or personality of the characters. Moreover, decorative patterns are added to the forehead and the space between the brows.

The "three-tile face with flowery patterns" is mainly used to depict a strutting military officer. All such characters wear stage armor (made of silk and embroidered back and front). The stage armor and the facial pattern form a perfect contrast and give a more vivid expression to the personality of the character.

三、花三块瓦脸

在各色三块瓦脸的基础上，对眉、眉窝、眼窝、鼻窝各部分用更细致、更丰富的手法，勾画出切合人物性格的不同图案，在额头、印堂部位增加了装饰性的图形，这就形成了丰富多彩，富于变化的各式"花三块瓦脸"。

花三块瓦脸的色彩基调仍保持各色三块瓦脸的寓意和象征，绘花三块瓦脸的人物以凶猛、粗放的武将居多，一般都"扎靠"穿铠甲。服装、脸谱相映成辉，斑斓绚丽。

23

(chart 3)（谱式3）

㉙ Xiahou Yuan in *Dingjun Mountain*. Xiahou Yuan is a general under Cao Cao in operas based on stories of the Three Kingdoms Period.

Black three-tile face with flowery patterns: The warped eyes and nostrils, the broken Chinese character for "longevity" and the disorderly lines all serve to signify that this man is doomed to die early.

《定军山》之夏侯渊，三国戏中曹操麾下大将。

黑花三块瓦脸，翘曲的眼窝、鼻窝，面中残断的寿字，散碎的线条，勾画出这位短命武夫的形象。

㉚ Cao Hong in *Changbanpo*. Cao Hong was a general under Cao Cao in operas based on stories of the Three Kingdoms Period.

Red three-tile face with flowery patterns: Changeable curved lines form a motif in the space between the brows. The red and black colors form a contrast and are intermingled with yellow and white lines, producing a sort of lively harmony.

《长坂坡》之曹洪，三国戏中曹操麾下战将。

红花三块瓦脸，眉眼间以富于变化的曲线组成图案，红黑相衬，间以黄白线条，和谐中有跳跃感。

25

③1 Dou Erdun, a fugitive in *Stealing the Royal Horse*.

Blue three-tile face with flowery patterns: The cheeks are blue and the forehead is given a flowery motif, with the ridge of the nose painted in intermingled red and white. In the space between the eyebrows is a pattern resembling the hooks which he uses as weapons. All this is meant to give him the image of a hero of the greenwood.

《盗御马》中之绿林英雄窦尔敦。

蓝花三块瓦脸，蓝靛脸，花眉窝，鼻梁红白相间，印堂悬胆突出，眉间画出其所用兵器护手双钩图样，一幅草莽英雄形象。

(32) Dian Wei, a general under Cao Cao, in *The Battle of Wancheng City.*

Yellow three-tile face with flowery patterns: Flaring red eyebrows indicate ferocity. In the area around the temples are painted images of his favorite weapons—two short-handled halberds. The red dot between the eyebrows indicates that he is extremely loyal to his master.

《战宛城》之典韦，三国戏曹操麾下战将。

黄花三块瓦脸，眼窝透出凶气，旋转的红眉，眉窝中专门画了典韦制胜无敌的兵器 — 双戟，印堂一点红心，显示了他对主人的忠贞。

33 Gao Deng, the villain in *Sunny Mansion*.

Three-tile face with flowery patterns on an oily white base: Curved brows, deep eye sockets and upturned canthuses and nostrils in an oily white face vividly depict the peremptory and overbearing image of a vicious young gangster.

《艳阳楼》之恶霸高登。

油白花三块瓦脸，眉窝弯曲，眼窝下垂，眼角上吊，油光粉面，鼻孔上翻，一副横蛮霸道的恶少面孔。

34 Xu Shiying in *Sunny Mansion*.

Green three-tile face with flowery patterns: Green forehead, flowery nostrils and inflated mouth in a pinkish face vividly convey the tempestuous nature of a wild young man.

《艳阳楼》之徐世英。

绿花三块瓦脸。绿额头，花鼻窝，粉面颊，翘嘴巴，生动刻画了粗卤、暴躁的青年武士神气。

㉟ Ximen Bao in *Ximen Bao*. Ximen Bao was a famous statesman in the Warring States Period (475–221 B.C.).

Purple three-tile face with flowery patterns: Up-turned black eyebrows against a crescent-shaped white supercilium, nostrils thickly painted white as well as sharp column-like vertical lines together produce the image of a honest and resourceful local official.

《西门豹》之西门豹，为战国时期著名政治家。

紫花三块瓦脸，上挑的黑眉相衬的月牙形白眉窝，宽而重的鼻窝，鲜明的立柱纹，共同组合成一个正直、多谋的地方长官的威严形象。

28

㊱ Lian Bo in *The General and the Premier Make Up*. Lian Bo was a famous general in the Warring States Period (475–221 B.C.).

Three-tile face with flowery patterns for characters advanced in age: Protuberant forehead, outer eye corners decorated with cloud patterns and pinkish cheeks indicate good health in advanced age and produce a kind of vigorous and dignified air.

《将相和》之廉颇，为战国时期的著名战将。

老花三块瓦脸。眉端突起，眼角垂云，粉红面颊，鹤发童颜。苍劲中有一股威武正气。

㊲ Sagacious Lu (Lu Zhishen) in *The Forest of Wild Boars*. Sagacious Lu is the monk hero in operas adapted from stories from the classic novel Outlaws of the Marsh.

A typical facial pattern specially reserved for monks and Taoists, it is developed from the three-tile face with flowery patterns. The thick brows indicate valor; the narrow and long eye sockets are meant to depict the mien of holy men when chanting the scriptures, while the round red dot between the brows signifies a Buddhist relic, which is the most characteristic feature of the facial patterns for monks.

《野猪林》之鲁智深，水浒传戏中僧人，后加入义军。

属于僧道脸谱一类。是由花三块瓦脸衍变而来，粗眉以示勇武，窄细的眼窝酷似诵经时的神态；额中间一点红圆光名为舍利珠，是和尚脸的特色。

(38) **Zhou Cang in *Huarong Path*.** Zhou Cang was adjutant general under Guan Yu's command in operas based on stories from the Three Kingdoms Period (220–265).

Silver ingot-shaped face with flowery patterns: This facial pattern is developed on the basis of the silver ingot-shaped face and three-tile face with flowery patterns, featuring bat-like patterns around the nose ridge and eye sockets against sharp white lines. A sort of harmony and liveliness emerges from the contrast.

《华容道》之周仓，三国戏中蜀国大将关羽的部将。

花元宝脸，由元宝脸和花三块瓦脸发展而来，鼻梁与眼窝组成酷似蝙蝠的图案，几道鲜明的白线相衬，对比中有和谐，活泼耐看。

IV. *Liu Fen Lian* (Six-Section Face)

Also called *lao lian* (old face), the "six-section face" derives from the "prepared face," only maintaining the major color on the cheeks. A colored area that is wide at top and narrow down below runs from the top of the nose to the forehead, and the whitened part around the eye sockets is extended to cover half of the forehead, while the black eyebrows are simplified into two gray oval dots. The relatively large area of white color forms a clear contrast with the main color on the cheeks. The design is simple yet solemn, suitable for revered veteran military officers, kings, nobles, etc.

Seemingly simple, the "six-section" facial pattern is very difficult to draw-the two curved lines have to be appropriate and in perfect harmony with the different types of faces of the actors.

四、六分脸

也称老脸，由整脸演变而来，谱中保留了两颊的主色，鼻端至脑门留下一条上宽下窄的色带。把白眉窝部分扩大到半面额头，而把黑眉简化为两个椭圆形的灰色点。大面积白色与两颊主色形成鲜明对比。构图简洁、庄重，很适宜表现德高望重、老当益壮的武将王侯一类角色。

六分脸谱式看似简单，勾画时要求很高，两条曲线在不方不圆中变化，并结合演员脸型特征做到恰到好处，很不容易。

(chart 4) （谱式4）

32

㊴ Huang Gai in *A Meeting of Heroes*. Huang Gai is a general of the Kingdom of Wu in operas based on stories from the Three Kingdoms Period (220–265).

The character has a red six-section face. In the opera, Huang Gai fakes surrender to Cao Cao, commander of the Wei troops, after volunteering to undergo a flogging by Zhou Yu, commander of the Wu troops, indicating the old general's ardent loyalty to his own country.

《群英会》之黄盖，三国戏中吴国大将。

红六分脸，黄盖曾以苦肉计诈降曹操。表现了一个老将军精忠报国的献身精神。

(40) Yuchi Gong in *The Imperial Orchard*. Yuchi Gong was a general who helped to found the Tang Dynasty.

Black six-section face: The white nose ridge is a unique feature of the black six-section face. The sharp contrast between black and white plays a positive role in depicting the character's stouthearted, brave and valiant disposition.

《御果园》之尉迟恭，唐朝开国将军。

黑六分脸，白鼻梁是不同于其他六分脸的特点。黑白分明对表现人物刚毅、勇敢、威武的性格特征起到了很好的作用。

34 Li Keyong (856-908) in *The State of Shatuo*. Li Keyong was the king of a tribe in northwest China during the Tang Dynasty (618–907).

The red six-section face suggests the image of a noble and courageous tribal king. The three red marks are said to represent wounds caused by an eagle's claws.

《沙陀国》之李克用（公元856－908年），唐代中国西北方的一个部落番王。

红六分脸，刻画了一个富贵、威武的番王形象。额上三道红印据传是曾被雕爪抓伤的痕迹，形成了李克用脸谱特有的记征。

34

42 Xu Yanzhao in *Entering the Palace for the Second Time*. Xu was said to have been a much-respected noble of the Ming Dynasty who selflessly guarded the interests of the state and showed great concern for the people.

Xu Yanzhao has a purple six-section face. Legend has it that the Xu family was loyal to the imperial court for generations and had a martial tradition. The purple color signifies loyalty, while the official cap and bronze hammers in his hands imply his military prowess.

《二进宫》之徐延昭，明代传说中护国安民的定国王侯。

紫六分脸，徐家世代忠良，且尚武家风。紫色寓有忠义、威武之意，配以公侯帽和铜锤，十分威严稳重。

V. *Shi Zi Men Lian* (Cross-Shaped Face)

The "cross-shaped face" is developed on the basis of the "three-tile face" and "six-section face" by joining the eye sockets of the "three-tile face" with the vertical color belt of the "six-section face" at the point between the eyebrows, hence its name. This type of face charts give prominence the forehead and nose, producing a more three-dimensional feeling impression of the face.

On the basis of the "cross-shaped face," the white area around the eye sockets can be widened a bit to look like a bird's wings; together with the black ridge of the nose, the whole face looks like that of a magpie. Therefore, this type of face design is popularly known as the "magpie-eyed face." If the eye sockets and nostrils are painted, the whole pattern of the face will turn into a butterfly with extended wings. Changing the colors on the forehead and between the eyebrows will produce a flowery butterfly face.

五、十字门脸

十字门脸谱是在三块瓦脸和六分脸的基础上发展演变而来。它把三块瓦脸的眼窝和六分脸的垂直色带在印堂处交成十字，所以叫十字门脸。这种谱式突出了隆起的脑门和鼻端，使得面部更具立体感。

在十字门脸的基础上，把眼窝加宽画成形似鸟的翅膀，衬上白鼻梁上相交的黑十字，活像一只喜鹊，这种用于活泼暴躁人物上的谱示俗称喜鹊眼脸。把黑眼窝与鼻窝相连又变化出宛然一幅蝴蝶剪影的蝴蝶脸，调整额头、眉窝的颜色又演变出复杂的花蝴蝶脸。

(chart 5) （谱式 5）

43 **Yao Qi in *Caoqiao Pass***. Yao Qi was a renowned general who helped to found the Eastern Han Dynasty (125-220).

Cross-shaped face for old characters: The eye sockets turn up slightly, and at the corners of the eyes there are bead-like patterns. Together with pinkish cheeks and wide nostrils, the pattern demonstrates the vigor and steadiness of the general in advanced age.

《草桥关》之姚期，东汉（公元123 - 220年）时期的开国大将。

十字门老脸，眼窝微挑、眼角垂珠、面颊粉红、鼻窝宽厚，表现将军暮年苍劲，稳重的神态。

(44) Xiang Yu in *The King's Parting with His Favorite*. Xiang Yu led a peasant uprising, and later proclaimed himself Conqueror of Western Chu at the end of the Qin Dynasty (221–207 B.C.).

The facial pattern for the character Xiang Yu is unique. The two brows are uneven and disorderly, and the eye sockets hang down, vividly depicting the tragic image of a great hero.

《霸王别姬》之项羽,秦(公元前221–前207年)末起义军领袖,后自立为西楚霸王。

项羽的脸谱独具持色。两道寿字眉参差散乱;眼窝低垂一付哭容,绘就了这个悲剧人物的英雄形象。

38

㊺ Meng Liang in *Muke Stronghold*. Meng Liang is a warrior in operas about the Yang family generals of Song Dynasty (960–1279).

The face is painted to resemble a magpie, developed on the basis of the cross-shaped face, with the eye sockets painted in the shape of the outspread wings. Legend has it that Meng Liang uses a gourd that shoots out flames as a weapon. Therefore, the space between the two wings is delineated into the shape of a red gourd. Together with red cheeks, beard and armor, the image is that of the god of fire.

《穆柯寨》之孟良,《杨家将》戏曲中战将。

喜鹊眼脸,由十字门脸发展而成,眼窝勾画成飞起喜鹊翅状;传说孟良有火葫芦做兵器,故中间垂直色带变为红色葫芦形状;两颊衬以红色,再加上红胡子,红铠甲犹如火神形象。

46 Jiao Zan in *Muke Stronghold*. Jiao Zan is also a warrior in operas about the Yang family generals of the Song Dynasty and always forms a pair with Meng Liang.

A typical magpie pattern: Black eye sockets and white nasal ridge form a sharp contrast, looking like a magpie with its wings extended. This facial pattern is appropriate for hotheaded yet simple and honest roles.

《穆柯寨》之焦赞。

典型的喜鹊眼脸，黑眼窝，白鼻梁，黑白相间，像展开双翅的喜鹊，活泼跳跃。此形象很适于急躁又憨态十足的人物。

孟良，焦赞在舞台上经常同时出场，一黑一红，十分醒目。

40

⑽ Zhang Fei in *Romance of Liu Bei and Sun Shangxiang*. Zhang Fei is cast as a brave general of the Kingdom of Shu in operas based on stories of the Three Kingdoms Period.

A butterfly face developed on the basis of a cross-shaped face: The eye sockets are wide and turn up, and the nostrils are almost linked with the eye sockets, looking like a butterfly. There is stress on the protruding forehead and round eyes, thus giving the character a humorous and joyful image, and hinting at an honest and outspoken disposition.

《龙凤呈祥》之张飞，三国戏中蜀国猛将。

蝴蝶脸，由十字门脸发展而来。眼窝宽大而上挑，鼻窝儿几乎与眼窝相连，正是蝴蝶的剪影，因故得名。谱中还突出人物豹头环眼的特征，在刚直爽快中有一种诙谐的喜相。

㊽ Zhou Chu in *The Return of the Prodigal*. Zhou Chu is a young evil-doer who later repents and helps local people expel two demons.

A butterfly face: the hooked pattern between the brows is vertical, indicating chivalry, while the flowery nasal pits and up-turned nostrils hint at his rascally aspect. The purple and red forehead indicates that he stops doing evil and turns over a new leaf.

《除三害》之周处。

蝴蝶脸，周处是为害乡里经调教改邪归正并为地方除害的人。眉间勾形纹直竖显示他打虎斩蛟的骁勇、花鼻窝、翻鼻孔的恶像显示他耍无懒的一面。紫印堂、红脑门是对他弃恶从善的肯定。

㊾ Li Kui in *Li Kui Visits His Mother*. Li Kui is a hero in operas adapted from the classical novel *Outlaws of the Marsh*.

A butterfly face: the eye sockets and nasal pits form a well-balanced pattern of a black butterfly. The forehead is generally black and in its middle is a red spot spouting three flames, depicting the simple and honest, upright and outspoken but somewhat rough image of a hero.

《李逵探母》之李逵，水浒传戏中梁山好汉。

蝴蝶脸、眼窝与鼻窝构成匀称的黑蝴蝶图案，黑脑门衬托出内画三簇火苗的红印堂，刻画了憨厚、刚直又粗卤的英雄形象。

㊿ Niu Gao in *Niu Gao Marries into His Bride's Family*. Niu Gao was a general of the Southern Song Dynasty (1127-1279) fighting against the invading Jin army. He defeated the enemy several times by trickery.

A butterfly face: the painting of the eye sockets and nasal pits produces a smiling face, and the well-delineated forehead discloses some astuteness in a generally upright and outspoken character.

《牛皋招亲》之牛皋。

南宋（公元 1127－1279 年）抗金将领。因智取敌将而立功。蝴蝶脸，笑眼窝，笑鼻窝满面喜气，秀气的眉窝在刚直豪爽中又透出一点机敏。

VI. *Hua Sui Lian* (Flowery Face with Broken Patterns) and Wai lian (Deformed Face)

The "flowery face with broken patterns" is developed on the basis of the "flowery three-tile face" and "flowery butterfly face." To appear flowery, broken and crinkled is the basic feature of this kind of facial pattern. Generally, curved lines are applied to the forehead, the eyes and eyebrows as well as the cheeks, to produce rich and varied patterns. Usually, one color is taken as the base and is mixed with many other auxiliary colors to produce a gorgeous effect.

The "deformed face" is derived from the "flowery face with broken patterns." Mainly used for those characters who have disfigured facial features, it possesses a more obvious nature of exaggeration.

With the exception of a very few cases in which the "flowery face with broken patterns" and the "deformed face" are rarely used for leading roles, they are usually used for ugly supporting roles portraying unpleasant people or members of a general's retinue.

六、花碎脸与歪脸

花碎脸是在花三块瓦脸、蝴蝶脸的基础上变化发展而来。花、碎、皱是这类脸谱的特征。一般在脑门、眉眼和两颊部分以细碎的曲线堆成变化丰富的图案。在一种主色中配以多种颜色的调合对比产生斑斓的效果。

歪脸是在花碎脸的基础上一种特殊的变化，主要用于那些五官不正畸形异貌的角色。形式上的不对称，更富夸张性。

花碎脸、歪脸除个别情况下用于剧中主要角色，一般多用于相貌丑的配角或武将护卫等。但因谱示复杂，演出中满台花花绿绿，能达到烘托气氛的效果。

43

(chart 6) （谱式6）

44

(51) Seventh Brother Yang in *The Banquet Ambush*. He is thus called because he is the seventh brother of the famous Yang family warriors of the Song Dynasty.

Black face with broken patterns: What is most typical of this facial pattern is the character meaning "tiger" in the middle of the forehead. The contrast formed by black and white is striking; it implies the valor as well as loyalty of a heroic general who is executed after trumped-up charges against him.

《金沙滩》之杨七郎，杨家将戏曲人物。

黑碎脸，最为典型的是脑门正中的一笔虎字。黑白相间柔中寓刚，十分醒目，象征这位被奸臣暗害，勇猛威武，忠于国家，威震敌胆的将军的精神。

(52) He Yuanqing in *Battle at Zhuxian Town*. He Yuanqin was a general under Yue Fei, a hero of the Southern Song Dynasty who led the resistance against the invading Jin army.

Red face with broken patterns. On the stage, He Yuanqing is very powerful; he wields two big staves and fights fiercely with Lu Wenlong, a young Jin general and the son of a Song general who had been killed by Jin troops. Their fight takes place before Lu gets to know the story of his father's fate. Lu later revolts against Jin and serves Yue Fei

《八大锤》之何元庆。

红碎脸，何元庆是南宋岳飞手下猛将，力大无比，在舞台上他手持双锤大战陆文龙，与少年英俊的陆文龙恰成鲜明的对比。

53 Xiahou De in *Dingjun Mountain*. Xiahou De is a hot-tempered but wit-less general under the command of Cao Cao in operas based on stories of the Three Kingdoms Period.

Blue face with bro-ken patterns. In the opera, Xiahou De is killed by Zhang Fei.

《定军山》之夏侯德，三国戏中曹操麾下战将。

绿碎脸，一个暴躁而有勇无谋的武夫，在定军山战役中一战毙命。

54 Shan Xiongxin in *Selling the Horse.* Shan Xiongxin is a hero in operas based on stories from the Sui Dynasty (581–618).

Blue face with broken patterns. A cold blue face with double-hooked brows, forehead with curved patterns and lion-like eye sockets are used to depict a fierce-looking hero who is fearless in the face of death.

《秦琼卖马》之单雄信，隋代传说戏曲人物。

蓝碎脸，双勾的眉毛，额头飘浮勾曲的花纹，狮子般的眼窝，阴冷的蓝色，刻画了这位凶神一般，威震绿林的英雄。

48

⑤⑤ Ma Wu in *Caoqiao Pass*. Like Yao Qi mentioned above, Ma Wu was also a general who helped to found the Eastern Han Dynasty (125−220).

Blue face with broken patterns. On the forehead is an articulated vertical pattern like the tail of a tiger. Together with it, the antler−like red brows and broken patterns on the cheeks vividly portray the disposition of a hero who is ugly in appearance but well versed in martial arts.

《草桥关》之马武，东汉开国武将。

兰碎脸，额头旋转有节的立柱酷似老虎尾巴，鹿角形红眉，面颊碎皱的花纹，既丑且凶，鲜明地刻画了这位外形丑陋、而武艺高强的英雄的性格。

56 Zheng En in *The Ex-ecution of General Zheng En*. Zheng En (or Zheng Ziming) was a romantic figure among the founders of the Song Dynasty (960–1279).

Deformed face. Zheng En's face was mauled by a wild animal when he defended its victim. Leg-end has it that he is the reincarnation of a blue dragon. This explains the whirling pattern on his forehead.

《斩黄袍》之郑子明。

歪斜脸，郑子明是宋朝开国元勋中一位传奇人物。因在山中救人，面部被野兽抓伤，致使五官变形。传说他是苍龙转世，所以其脸谱中眼分雌雄，脑门图案盘曲。

49

50

⑤⑦ Wang Bochao in *Jiepai Pass*. Wang was a general of an anti-Tang army.

Deformed face (also called "weeping face"), it signifies that the character usually brings back luck to others.

《界牌关》之王伯超。

歪斜脸，这个谱式又称哭丧脸，唐朝大将罗通伤于王伯超枪下。所以这种谱式多用于给人带来不祥之恶运的人物。

⑤⑧ Jin Wuzhu in *Overturning the Chariots*. Jin Wuzhu is the commander-in-chief of the Jin troops invading the Southern Song.

Flowery face with broken patterns. While the gold color implies the noble background of the character, the exaggerated eye sockets and mouth hint at some flaw in his nature, while at the same time indicating honesty and straightforwardness.

《挑滑车》之金兀术。

花碎脸，金色显示其异族首领的高贵身分。但眼窝，嘴形都颇为夸张，在丑化的同时又表现出人物的憨直。

52

⑤⑨ Zhong Wuyan in *The Concubine General*. Zhong Wuyan was a concubine of King Xuan of Qi in the Spring and Autumn Period (C.770-476 B.C.).

This is the only facial pattern for a female role in Peking and Kun operas. The story goes that, although Zhong Wuyan was well-versed in martial arts and had done great service for the state, King Xuan still cold-shouldered her because she was ugly. Yet, when the king and the state were threatened by danger, Zhong forgot her enmity against the king and came to his rescue.

《棋盘会》之钟无盐，春秋（约公元前770－前476年）时期齐宣王的王妃。

这是一个京剧、昆曲剧目中罕见的勾脸的女性角色，其剧情是说钟元盐面貌丑陋但武艺高强，虽然平时齐宣王冷落她，但在齐宣王危难时她不计前嫌，为国解危。

VII. *Shen Guai Lian* (Ghostly Face)

In the repertoire of Peking opera, there are many works based on fairy tales and ghost stories. This gives the actors the scope to bring into full play the exaggerative and symbolic means of presentation of Peking opera facial designs.

For immortals and celestial beings, usually the "flowery three-tile face" is taken as the base, with gold or silver highlights. More often than not, some motifs that are normally reserved for the roles of immortals and ghosts are painted on the forehead or cheeks.

There is also a type of facial pattern called *xiang xing lian* (pictographic face). It is derived from the "flowery face with broken patterns" and such motifs as birds, animals, scales and claws are added. This type of facial pattern is usually used for inhuman roles like animals and birds. The pictographic face chart is also applied to the roles of petty demons, which are presented as ugly.

七、神怪脸

京剧剧目中神话戏很多，在神怪角色的领域里，京剧脸谱夸张、象征的手法可以得到淋漓尽致的发挥。

神仙脸，以花三块瓦脸为基础施以金、银，在额头和面颊常常绘有神怪特殊符号的图案。

象形脸，借鉴花碎脸的形式加以变形，辅以鸟、兽、鳞、爪等精灵图案，如二十八宿、百鸟谱等。

小妖脸，多以象形的手法处理，以丑恶形象的居多。

53

(chart7)（谱式 7）

54

(60) The God Erlang in *Feast of Peaches*. According to the classical novel *Journey to the West*, True Lord Erlang (called Yang Jian) is the one who helps the heavenly generals defeat Sun Wukong the Monkey King.

Three-tile face on a golden base: The character has one more eye in the middle of the forehead, producing a ferocious yet noble appearance that is suited to his position as a commander of the heavenly soldiers.

《蟠桃会》之二郎神，神话小说《西游记》中众天神之一。

金色地三块瓦脸，脑门中多生一目，高贵中有一股杀气威凛的怒容。符合其天兵主帅的身分。

61 **The Monkey King in** *Havoc in Heaven*. The Monkey King is the leading character in the classical novel *Journey to the West*.

The entire face is painted in the shape of an inverted peach, with two fiery and shining eyes to express the character's wit and attraction.

《大闹天宫》之孙悟空，神话小说《西游记》的主角。

一个倒置桃子的形象，两道闪着金光的火眼金睛，俏皮活泼，十分可爱。

(62) Mighty Miracle God, one of the heavenly generals in *Havoc in Heaven.*

On the stage, the character is clumsy and doltish. The facial pattern is characterized by a large mouth, upturned nostrils and two heads, one upon the other. The character looks savage, but also rather ridiculous.

《闹天宫》之巨灵神，神话小说《西游记》中众神灵之一。

舞台上的巨灵神硕大，呆笨。脸谱为大嘴巴，翻鼻孔，头上又生一人头，看起来凶恶，蛮横，更有几分可笑。

(63) The Bull Devil King in *Water Curtain Cave.*

A golden flowery face with broken patterns featuring red brows, flowery eye sockets and upturned nostrils. The two hooks painted on the forehead signify the horns of a violent bull.

《水帘洞》之牛魔王，神话小说《西游记》中众妖魔之一。

金黄花碎脸，红眉毛，花眼窝，翘鼻窝，翻鼻孔。额头双勾象征牛角，神似凶猛的公牛。

64 The Leopard Demon in *The Leopard Demon*.
The Leopard Demon is one of the numerous demons and monsters that appear in *Journey to the West*.

The facial pattern places primary stress on depicting the ravenous image of a fierce leopard by painting the brows white, highlighting the eyes and painting the mouth blood-red. The spots on both sides of the face are mainly for decoration.

《金钱豹》之豹精，神话小说《西游记》中众魔之一。

白眉凶目，血盆大嘴，一幅凶恶残忍的豹子头像。两颊辅以金钱图案，更具有装饰性。

65 The Dragon King of the East Sea in *Havoc in Heaven*, adapted from *Journey to the West*.

In the novel, the dragon is the leader of the dragon kings of the four seas, and so he enjoys prestige. Therefore, the three-tile facial pattern is used for this character.

《闹龙宫》之东海龙王，神话小说《西游记》中神怪之一。

东海龙王为四海诸王之首，当属德高望重，故习惯上绘以老三块瓦脸的谱式。

66 The Plough God in the fairy tale opera *One Hundred People Enjoying Long Lives,* which is staged on auspicious occasions such as birthdays.

On the basis of the purple three-tile face, the pattern of the Plough is painted on the forehead, thus giving the character an air of solemnity and also serving to show that the character is a supernatural being.

神话戏《百寿图》之北斗星君。

吉庆剧目，多为贺寿之用。在紫三块瓦脸的基础上，脑门巧妙地绘成北斗七星的图案，既庄重，又具有神仙名分的明显标识。

⑥⑦ Zhong Kui in *Revenge for a Grave Wrong*. Zhong Kui is an upright figure in folk legends.

Flowery silver ingot-shaped face. It is said that Zhong Kui failed to pass the imperial civil service examination simply because his face had been disfigured by a mountain monster. After he died of grief, the Jade Emperor made him a god in charge of dispelling ghosts. As people believe that Zhong Kui can bring peace and happiness to them, the character bears the imprint of a bat (pronounced "fu" in Chinese, which is a homophone for "happiness"). The decoration of the brows and eyes signifies a kind of quietness in movement and beauty in ugliness.

《奇冤报》之钟馗，民间传说中传奇人物。

花元宝脸，传说他被山妖毁了容而未能中状元，感愤而死。死后被玉皇大帝敕封为驱除鬼魅的神灵。民间认为钟馗能给人们带来平安与福音。有的在脸谱上脑门有蝠，眉眼含俏，动中有静，丑中有美。

⑥⑧ The Judge of the Underworld.

Legend has it that this judge wields a red brush to decide the fates of all people. The base of the facial pattern can be in one of various different colors — black, red, blue, white, etc., which is then dotted with gold or silver, giving the character a grotesque appearance. The judge is a character in many operas.

"判官"是阴曹地府掌管审判文牍的官员，一支朱笔，世人生死由他。

其脸谱以黑、红、蓝、白等不同底色，点缀金银，形象勾画十分恐怖怪诞。在许多戏中都可见到这个角色。

VIII. *Chou Jue Lian* (Clown's Face)

In Peking opera, there are strict rules for the facial patterns of both the *jing* (painted face) and *chou* (clown) roles. The facial patterns for clownish roles are simpler than those for *jing* roles, and the facial area to be painted is also relatively smaller. Usually, black is used to delineate the sense organs, then white is applied to the part between the eyes, and the nose and mouth, to form square, kidney or date stone shapes for different roles. The major types of such roles are: (1) Civil clowns—mostly low-ranking officials, petty scholars, advisers to officials or profligate sons of rich families; (2) Old clowns—mostly steady, kind-hearted, witty and humorous old males; (3) Martial clowns—mostly warriors who are well versed in fighting skills as well as being sharp-witted and resourceful; and (4) Little clowns—mostly childish youngsters. In addition, there is another type, that is, rogues and local ruffians. The images of such people are usually ungainly and their facial drawings are casual. Furthermore, there are ugly and clownish old women and maids, for whom the emphasis is placed on their vulgarity in the facial designs.

八、丑角脸

京剧的行当中，净、丑角色都要依谱化妆。丑角脸谱比净角简单，勾画面积也较小，但更具特征。一般以黑色勾画五官，在眼鼻口之间部位用白色画成"豆腐块"、"腰子脸"、"枣核脸"等图案，适用于不同角色。常见的丑角有如下四种。文丑：多扮演将相官员，文人谋士或一些纨绔子弟等。老丑：多扮演老诚善良诙谐幽默的老年人。武丑：多扮演武艺高强灵巧机敏武士。小丑：多扮演未成年的儿童。另有一类是下层的恶棍地痞小人物，形象丑陋，化妆也相应随便。丑婆、丑丫头是由丑行应工的又一类有特色的人物，重在表现其粗俗的一面。

(chart 8) （谱式 8）

61

   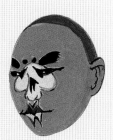

⑥⑨ Jiang Gan in *Meeting of Heroes*. Jiang Gan is a figure in operas adapted from stories of the Three Kingdoms Period (220–280).

A typical civilian clown, the character's face is painted with a white square, and his eyes and brows are lightly delineated. This pattern is primarily aimed at showing the foolishness and snobbishness of a bookworm.

《群英会》之蒋干，三国戏中人物。

典型的文丑，也称方巾丑，面上涂白豆腐块，眉眼轻描，于丑中透出秀气，重在刻画读书人的呆气和酸腐气。

⑦⓪ Wang Hui in *The Women Generals of the Yang Family*.

Wang Hui is a weak-kneed and muddle-headed high court official. As this character is advanced in age and displays an air of pedantry, his face is painted with a white square, and on the forehead are added several white wrinkles. His brows are white and inverted, and his eyes are diamond-shaped.

《杨门女将》之王辉。

身居高位，软弱糊涂的朝臣，涂白豆腐块，几笔白皱纹，倒白眉，棱形眼，苍老中更有一股迂腐气。

⑦① The little monk in *Getting Down the Mountain*.

This is a clown character in a short humorous opera which tells the story of a young monk and nun who elope from a monastery. The facial pattern features a white spot on the nasal ridge, while the rest of the face remains clean and rosy, showing that he is a lively but naughty young lad.

《下山》之小和尚。

小丑角，《下山》是一出寓庄于谐的小喜剧。写一僧一尼逃离寺院中途相遇的故事。其鼻梁一点白，脸色干净红润，俊秀中有顽皮，活泼中透出狡黠。

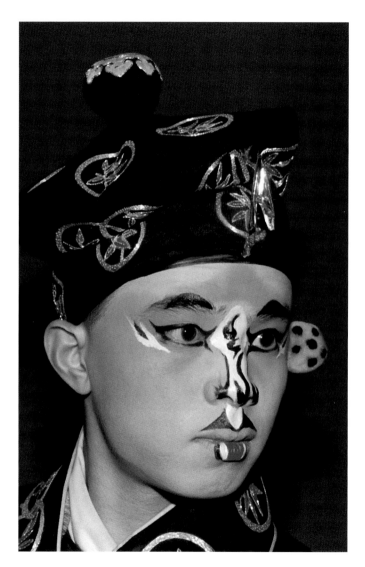

64

(72) Qin Ren in *Sunny Mansion*. Qin Ren is a hero who has a strong sense of justice.

A martial clown, he has a whitish facial pattern in the shape of a date stone. With only the corners of the mouth heavily delineated, he gives the impression of being extremely neat and agile.

《艳阳楼》之秦仁。

武丑，勾枣核形白脸，加勾嘴岔，干净利落，很有神气。

65

(73) The son of the villainous local official Yang in *Pavilion Overlooking the River*.

This young ruffian wears an official robe to reflect the power wielded by his father. His pinkish kidney-shaped face and crooked brows produce a repugnant stage image.

《望江亭》之杨衙内。

靠其父的势力披上官袍的恶少，勾腰子形粉脸，倒八字眉，形象令人厌恶。

(74) Chong Gongdao in *Courtesan Su San on Her Way to Court*. Chong is an aged court constable.

An old clown, he has a pinkish-white kidney-shaped face, with drooping white brows, small eyes, red lips and forehead, and white wrinkles, producing the image of a kind-hearted and humorous old man.

《女起解》之崇公道。

老丑，勾画白腰子粉脸，白八字眉，小圆眼，红嘴唇，额头、两颊和眼角画白皱纹，给人以善良风趣的感觉。

⑦⑤ Shi Qian in *Shi Qian Steals Some Chickens*, an opera adapted from the classical novel *Outlaws of the Marsh*.

On an irregularly shaped whitish face, this character has triangular eyes and a mouth that resembles a mouse, implying slyness. The short black beard implies chicken feathers.

《时迁偷鸡》之时迁，水浒传中梁山好汉。

异形白粉脸，三角眼，老鼠嘴。形象狡黠，寓意善盗。嘴边黑须，像是偷鸡留下的黑毛。

⑦⑥ Zhu Guangzu in *Lianhuantao*.

This martial clown has a powdered face in the shape of a date stone, with an inverted handle-bar mustache, giving the impression that the character is extremely sharp-witted and agile.

《连环套》之朱光祖。

武丑，勾枣核形粉脸，戴倒八字胡须，给人以非常机敏、灵活的感觉。

(77) Matchmaker Liu in *Picking Up the Jade Bracelet*.

An ugly, vulgar yet humorous female role in Peking Opera, it is usually performed by a man, with powder applied to the face, and the eyes and eyebrows lightly painted. In most cases, a mole is added to the face.

《法门寺》之衙役。

衙门中的差役，欺下媚上的小人物。勾腰子形粉脸，枣核眼，黑鼻头令人生厌。

(78) Xiahou Shang in *Dingjun Mountain*. Xiahou Shang was a general under Cao Cao.

In this opera, he is pitiful in defeat, yet humorous.

《定军山》之夏侯尚。

跻身大将行列，一战大败而归，如此装束，如此兵器，紧张的战争中尚不忘幽默，也属京剧艺术的特色之一。

⑲ **An ugly old woman**

This kind of facial pattern is usually reserved for servant woman working for rich families. They are either sly or honest and straightforward. Their head-gear and facial make-up have also become gradually stylized.

《拾玉镯》之刘媒婆。

　　此为丑婆，是丑角应工的另一类特色人物。以男性扮演一些粗俗滑稽的中老年妇女，面部略施朱粉，描绘眉眼、点画丑痣，突出其丑、俗、诙谐的特征。

⑳ **A constable in** *Famen Temple*.

In the olden days, constables attached to local government offices were bullies toward the common people and toadies to their masters. This character has a powdered face in the shape of a kidney. With date-stone-like eyes and a black nose, he has a repulsive air.

《丑丫头》一般为大户人家个性鲜明的婢女。

　　她们或是机敏圆滑，或是憨直愚钝，往往在剧情里起着推波助澜的作用。其在头饰和面部的化妆上也趋于程式化。

Synopses of Some Peking Operas

Picture 13: *Meeting of the Heroes*

A century-old item based on stories from the famous classical novel *Romance of the Three Kingdoms*. The story tells how in 208 A.D., Cao Cao, who was then the prime minister of the Eastern Han (25–220 A.D.) imperial court, led an expedition against the State of Wu (which had not proclaimed itself a kingdom then). The State of Wu forged an alliance with the State of Shu, which was on the rise, to defeat the Eastern Han forces on the Yangtze River near Chibi (Red Cliffs), which is said to be within the boundaries of present-day Puqi City, Hubei Province. The opera is based on this episode, describing the meeting of generals and strategists of all three sides before the battle.

Picture 14: *Ganlu Temple*

Also based on a tale from the Three Kingdoms Period, the background to the opera is as follows: The State of Shu borrowed the strategic town of Jingzhou from the State of Wu and stationed troops. As Shu failed to return Jingzhou to the State of Wu for a long time, Sun Quan, king of the State of Wu, worked out a plan to marry his sister Sun Shangxiang to Liu Bei, king of Shu, as a trick to take the latter hostage. Liu's chief advisor Zhuge Liang saw through the scheme and convinced Sun's mother at Ganlu Temple that Liu Bei was worthy of being her son-in-law. Thus the beauty trap fell through and Liu Bei married Sun Quan's sister. The title of the opera derives from the fact that the major events took place in Ganlu Temple.

This opera is often staged together with *Returning to Jingzhou* and *The Reed-Bestrewn Marsh*. Together, the three operas are called *The Romance of Liu Bei and Sun Shangxiang* (see pictures 27 and 47). The last two episodes of the story tell how Liu Bei, after marrying Sun Shangxiang, was so contented with the comforts of married life that he was reluctant to return to Jingzhou. Zhao Yun, following Zhuge Liang's instructions, gave him the false report that Cao Cao's troops were planning an attack on Jingzhou, forcing him to return quickly. Sun Shangxiang followed her husband to Jingzhou without letting her mother and brother know.

Pictures 15 and 26: *The Empty City Ruse*

For about half century after the Battle of Chibi, the three kingdoms of Wei, Shu and Wu maintained a kind of power balance. But, Wei and Shu fought each other from time to time. In 228 A.D., Zhuge Liang, then prime minister of Shu, led an expedition to fight troops from Wei, ordering Ma Su, a principal general of Shu, to lead the vanguard of the Shu troops. But Ma Su was bull-headed, and did not follow Zhuge Liang's instructions. As a result, he lost the strategic pass of Jieting to Wei, which quickly advanced on Xicheng, where Zhuge Liang had his headquarters but without a strong army to defend him. In the face of great danger, Zhuge Liang remained cool-headed and worked out the "empty city ruse." He had all the four gates of the city opened, and he himself went up to the tower over the main city gate and played the zither. Seeing this, Sima Yi was sure that Zhuge Liang must have laid an ambush for him, so he ordered his army to retreat. With this respite, Zhuge Liang sent for reinforcements.

Normally, *The Empty City Ruse* is performed together with *Loss of the Strategic Pass of Jieting* (see

Picture 26) and *The Execution of General Ma Su.*

Picture 16: *Beating Yan Song*
Yan Song was a powerful and treacherous court official in the mid-16th century, during the Ming Dynasty. When he was in power, he manipulated state affairs, embezzled allocations for defense, and framed and persecuted fellow court officials. Because of his treacherous behavior, all upright people hated him. Once, he secretly ordered craftsmen to make a crown for him, in preparation for usurping the throne. His scheme was discovered by Zou Yinglong, an honest and upright court official, who worked out a plan to foil Yan Song's treachery.

Pictures 17 and 38: *Huarong Path*
Also an episode from *Romance of the Three Kingdoms*, the story goes like this: After the Battle of Chibi, Cao Cao flees, escorted by only 18 of his generals. When he reaches the Huarong Path, he runs into an ambush laid by Guan Yu. Seeing that there is little hope of escape, Cao Cao personally approaches Guan Yu and reminds the latter how kindly he had treated him on a previous occasion. As a result, Guan Yu lets him go.

Picture 18: *Escorting Jingniang Home*
This is a story about Zhao Kuangyin (929–976), who later became the founding emperor of the Song Dynasty. Zhao is a brave warrior who rescues a girl named Jingniang who had been kidnapped by a group of bandits. He makes the girl his sworn sister, and escorts her home for a thousand *li*. On the way, the girl falls in love with Zhao, and hints on many occasions how she feels. Yet, Zhao politely declines her approaches, for he thinks that it would be improper to seek a favor from someone he has saved.

Picture 19: *The Scholar's Wife* or *Execution of the Imperial Son-in-Law*
A long-established item in the repertoire of Peking Opera, the synopsis of the story is as follows: Chen Shimei, a scholar of the Northern Song Dynasty (960–1127), takes the imperial examination in the capital city, Bianliang (present-day Kaifeng in Henan Province), and passes top of the list. He conceals the fact that he is married and has one son and one daughter, so that he can marry the emperor's daughter. Three years later, his first wife, Qin Xianglian, comes to the capital to look for him, together with their children. Chen pretends not to know her, and orders his vassal Han Qi to kill them. But Han Qi is an upright man. Knowing that he will be punished if he disobeys his master and that he will suffer from a guilty conscience all his life if he commits the deed, he kills himself instead. Taking the knife as evidence, Qin Xianglian lodges a complaint against Chen Shimei with Bao Zheng, a much-praised upright court official. Consequently, the two confront each other in court. In the end, Bao Zheng has Chen executed in spite of pressure from the emperor's mother and sister.

Picture 20: *Famen Temple*
Liu Jin (?–1510) was a powerful court eunuch in the Ming Dynasty (1368–1644), and his treacherous influence and oppression were felt throughout the country. Yet, in this opera he appears as a defender of

justice.

The story goes like this: Matchmaker Liu acts as a go-between for a scholar and a girl. But the matchmaker's good-for-nothing son kills two of the girl's relatives in an attempt to frame the scholar, throwing the heads into the courtyard of a local official. The official, finding the heads, throws them into a well for fear of getting involved. However, he is also forced to kill a servant boy who witnessed his disposal of the evidence. The scholar is framed for the murders, but Liu Jin finally ferrets out the truth.

Pictures 21, 33 and 34: *Sunny Mansion*

This is an opera full of acrobatic fighting episodes. The simple story goes like this: In the Northern Song Dynasty (960-1179), Gao Deng, the dandy son of Gao Qiu, the powerful and treacherous prime minister, kidnaps Xu Peizhu, a beautiful young lady, takes her to Sunny Mansion and forces her to marry him. Upon hearing of this, the young lady's brother seeks help from martial arts masters Hua Fengchun, Qin Ren and Huyan Bao. They sneak into the mansion at night, kill Gao Deng to rescue the girl.

Picture 23: *Three Attacks on Zhu Family Village*

Shi Qian and some other greenwood heroes of the classical novel *Outlaws of the Marsh* stay at an inn set up by the Zhu family. They steal some chickens, and for this they are imprisoned and tortured by the Zhus. Their comrades on Mount Liangshan, led by Chao Gai, attack the village three times and finally succeed in rescuing the prisoners. A related opera piece is *Shi Qian Steals Some Chickens* (see Picture 75).

Pictures 24, 25 and 30: *Changbanbo*

This is another opera based on the novel *Romance of the Three Kingdoms*. The story goes like this: Cao Cao leads his army south, driving Liu Bei ahead of him. Liu Bei's family gets lost in the fierce fighting. Zhao Yun, one of Liu's generals, charges into the enemy ranks several times and manages to find Liu's wives—Lady Gan and Lady Mi—with his infant son. Lady Mi entrusts the baby to Zhao and kills herself by jumping into a well. Zhao Yun carries the baby in his bosom and fights his way to safety with the help of Zhang Fei, who comes to Zhao's aid at Changbanpo.

Picture 28: *The Mouth of the Jiujiang River*

In the mid-13th century, the Yuan Dynasty is rocked by peasant rebellions and natural disasters. Chen Youliang and Zhang Shicheng form an alliance against Zhu Yuanzheng, who later becomes the founding emperor of the Song Dynasty (1388-1644). Chen pledges to marry his daughter to Zhang's son to strengthen the ties between them. But Zhang's son is captured by Zhu Yuanzhang's troops in an ambush on his way to greet his fiancée. Then, one of Zhu's generals disguises himself as Chen's would-be son-in-law and leads Chen into an ambush. Zhang Dingbian, Chen's marshal, sees through the conspiracy and attempts to stop Chen, finally coming to his rescue at the mouth of the Jiujiang River by disguising himself as a fisherman.

Pictures 29, 53 and 78: *Dingjun Mountain*

Another opera adapted from *Romance of the Three Kingdoms*.

Huang Zhong, a leading general under Liu Bei, volunteers to lead an army to attack Cao Cao's stronghold on Dingjun Mountain. But he meets his match in Xiahou Yuan. Huang thereupon challenges Xiahou Yuan to a duel. Feigning flight, he lures Xiaohou Yuan to his death, and goes on to capture the stronghold.

Pictures 31 and 76: *Stealing the Royal Horse* (also titled *Lianhuantao*)

Dou Erdun, a *Robin Hood-like hero in the Qing Dynasty* (1644-1911), joins an outlaw band at Lianhuantao, in the remote mountainous region beyond the Great Wall. He is determined to get revenge on Huang Santai, who once injured him with a dart-like weapon. He steals a horse which had been bestowed on imperial marshal Deng Jiugong and implicates Huang in the theft. Huang Tianba, Huang Santai's son, is sent to investigate, and he finally clears his father' s name.

Picture 32: *Battle of Wancheng City*

This opera is based on story from the Three Kingdoms Period.

At the end of the Eastern Han Dynasty (25-220 A.D.), Cao Cao attacks the city of Wancheng (in present-day Henan Province). Zhang Xiu, the general guarding the city, surrenders without a fight. Yet, he rises against Cao Cao when the latter takes his aunt as a concubine. Having disarmed Dian Wei, the general leading Cao Cao' s bodyguards, Zhang Xiu launches a night attack. Dian Wei fights and dies a heroic death to protect Cao Cao, who narrowly escapes.

Picture 35: *Ximen Bao*

This opera is adapted from a Warring States Period (475-221 B.C.) story. The plot goes like this: In a place called Ye (now Yezhen Town in Linzhang County, Hebei Province) in the State of Wei, it was the custom to sacrifice young girls to the River God every year by throwing them into the river. When Ximen Bao is appointed the local magistrate, he decides to put an end to this barbaric superstition. When the time comes to find a new bride for the river god, he says that the girl chosen is not good enough, and orders that the local witch and tyrant to be thrown in the river to tell the river god another choice would be made. Thenceforth, a halt was put to this human sacrifice.

Picture 36: *The General and the Premier Make Up*

This opera is based on "The Biographies of Lian Bo and Lin Xiangru" in *Records of the Historian* by Sima Qian of the Han Dynasty. Written in the first century B.C., *Records of the Historian* is China's first history book, composed of biographies.

The leading characters in the opera are Lian Bo and Lin Xiangru of the State of Zhao in the Warring States Period (474-221 B.C.). When Lin Xiangru is made premier, a post higher than Lian Bo's, the latter is indignant and challenges Lin three times in the street. But Lin, putting the interests of the state above his own dignity, refuses to be provoked. Lian Bo, thereupon, is ashamed of his conduct, and goes to Lin's residence with a stick tied to his back, to ask for a flogging. The two then become goods friends, and help to make the State of Zhao a great power.

Picture 37: *The Forest of Wild Boars*

An episode from *Outlaws of the Marsh*, the opera tells the following story: In the Northern Song Dynasty

(960-1127), the dandy son of Gao Qiu, the defense minister, takes a fancy to the beautiful wife of Lin Chong, a military officer under Gao Qiu. The father and son get Lin sent into exile, and bribe the guards to murder him on the way. But Lin's sworn brother, a monk named Lu Zhishen (called "Sagacious Lu" in the novel) follows the party secretly, and saves Lin from death in the Forest of Wild Boars.

Picture 40: *The Imperial Orchard*

This opera tells a story about strife at the court of the Tang Dynasty (618-907). The two brothers of Li Shimin, later Emperor Taizong, accuse General Yuchi Gong of lying when he said that he had saved the life of the current emperor (Li Yuan). Both sides agree to reproduce the scene again in the imperial garden in front of many witnesses. It is in the depth of winter and exceptionally cold. Yuchi Gong takes a cold-resistant pill Li Jing (another general under Li Shiming) gives him, and re-enacts his meritorious feat.

Picture 42: *Entering the Palace for the Second Time*

In 1572, following the death of Emperor Muzhong of the Ming Dynasty, Imperial Concubine Li acts as regent for her infant son, managing state affairs from behind a screen. Li Liang, the concubine's father, attempts to usurp the throne. Xu Yanzhao (Duke Dingguo) and Yang Bo (vice minister of defense) go to the court twice to reason with the imperial concubine, and finally make her understand the situation. The imperial concubine asks them to assist the young emperor in government.

Picture 43 and 55: *Caoqiao Pass*

In the reign of Emperor Guangwu of the Eastern Han Dynasty (25-220 A.D.), Yao Qi, the general guarding Caoqiao Pass, is summoned back to the capital to take up another post. Yao Gang, Yao Qi's son, kills with his bare fists the emperor's father-in-law, who was trying to usurp the throne and bullying the rest of the officials. At this, the emperor orders the old general Yao Qi's whole family executed. Just at this critical juncture, enemy troops attack Caoqiao Pass, and the capital is threatened. Ma Wu, who has succeeded Yao Qi as the commander guarding the pass, rushes back to court for reinforcements. He persuades the emperor to rescind the execution order and send Yao Qi and his son on the mission to atone for their crime.

Picture 44: *The King's Parting with His Favorite*

A tragedy of love with the background of war, this opera tells how in 202 B.C. Xiang Yu, the Conqueror of Western Chu, and his troops are trapped by the troops of Liu Bang at Gaixia. Xiang Yu's wife Yu Ji, aware of the impossibility of breaking out of the encirclement, bids farewell to her husband and takes her own life in the hope of relieving the burden on her husband. Xiang Yu manages to get away. But he is so upset at losing his wife and being defeated, he also kills himself.

Pictures 45 and 46: *Muke Stronghold* or *Dragon-Subduing Wood*

This is one of the stories about the famous Yang family generals of the Northern Song Dynasty (960-1127). It goes like this: Yang Yanzhao, or Sixth Brother Yang, is commander-in-chief of a border garrison. The commander of the enemy troops sets up a "heavenly gate battle formation" and challenges

Yang to break it. Yang sends Meng Liang to ask his elder brother, Fifth Brother Yang, for assistance. Yet, his brother says that he needs a particular kind of wood, called "dragon-subduing wood," to make the handle of a battle-ax. It so happens that the wood can only be found in Muke Stronghold. Then, Yang Yanzhao sends Meng Liang and Jiao Zan to the stronghold for the wood. The two offend Mu Guiying and are beaten by her. They then instigate Yang Zongbao, Yang Yanzhao's son, to fight Mu Guiying. But Yang Zongbao is also captured. In the end, Yang Zongbao and Mu Guiying marry. This opera foreshadows another one, called *Mu Guiying Breaks the Heaven's Gate Battle Formation*.

Picture 48: *Return of the Prodigal*

Zhou Chu is orphaned at an early age and grows up a drunken bully. In his hometown of Yixing, he is considered the third scourge of the area along with a fierce tiger and a "flood dragon." Wang Jun, the county magistrate, thinks the young man can be educated and rehabilitated. Disguised himself as a senile old man, he waits for Zhou Chu by the roadside. He first taunts him by referring to the three scourges of the local people, and then has a heart-to-heart talk with him. Zhou is touched by the "old man's" sincerity and decides to turn over a new leaf. Finally, he kills the tiger and the dragon, ridding the place of all the scourges.

Picture 49: *Li Kui Visits His Mother*

Li Kui was a reckless but righteous and filial member of the outlaws on Mount Liangshan. In this opera, Li Kui gains permission from his leader, Song Jiang, to return home and see his mother. On his way home, he meets Li Gui, who has disguised himself as Li Kui to rob travelers. Li Kui gives him a good beating and wants to kill him. Li Gui lies that his family is so poor that he has to steal to feed his old mother. Li Kui is taken in, and gives the rascal some money. Reaching home, he is greatly grieved to see the dreadful plight his mother is in, and decides to take her back to the mountain with him. Having traveled some distance, his mother says she is thirsty. Li Kui goes to fetch some water. While he is away, two tiger cubs come and eat his mother. Enraged, Li Kui kills the two cubs and their parents.

Picture 51: *The Banquet Ambush*

The king of Liao (907-1125) invites Emperor Taizu (976-997) of the Song Dynasty to meet him at a place called Jinshatan for a summit between the two states. Yang Jiye, an old and resourceful general of the loyal Yang family, suspects a trap, and so he disguises his eldest son, Yang Yanping, as the emperor and sends his other seven sons to protect him. In the middle of a banquet, the Liao troops surround them. Yanping is killed after shooting the king of Liao to death with a short bow hidden in his sleeve. The second and third brothers fight to the death, the fourth and eighth brothers are captured by the enemy, while the fifth, sixth and seventh brothers break out of the siege.

Picture 52: *The Battle at Zhuxian Town*

In 1127, the Northern Song empire was toppled by the State of Jin established by Nüchens (later known as the Manchus) in northeast China. In the same year, the Southern Song Dynasty was established at Lin'an (now Hangzhou in Zhejiang Province). At the Southern Song court, some upright civil and military officials vow to resist Jin and recover the lost land. The famous general Yue Fei (1103–1142) led his Yue family army to defeat the Jin troops on many occasions. This opera reproduces the fierce struggle between He Yuanqing and three other generals of the Yue family army and the Jin general Lu Wenlong.

Picture 55: *The Execution of General Zheng En*

In 960, Zhao Kuangyin, originally a general of the Later Zhou Kingdom, seizes the throne with the support of Zheng En, Gao Huaide and some others, and becomes the first emperor of the Song Dynasty. To seek his favor, Han Long sends his sister Han Sumei to Zhao Kuangyin as an imperial concubine. Consequently, Han Sumei becomes a favorite of the emperor, and Han Long is also given a noble title and allowed to parade around the capital in official robes. When Zheng En runs into Han and sees his arrogance, he gives him a good beating out of indignation. Believing his concubine's slanderous tales, the drunken emperor orders Zheng En executed. Shocked by the news, Tao Sanchun, Zheng En's wife, lays siege to the imperial palace with her husband's troops. Sobering up, Zhao Kuangyin realizes that he has made a grave mistake and begs Gao Huaide to mediate. Having killed Han Long, Gao Huaide mounts the palace wall and tries to talk Tao Sanchun over. Finally, Tao lifts the siege, slashing the emperor's robe as a token gesture of revenge.

Picture 57: *Jiepai Pass*

In the early days of the Tang Dynasty (618–907), Emperor Taizong leads a punitive expedition against the tribes in the western frontier region, with Qin Huaiyu serving as the commander-in-chief. The enemy commander, Su Baotong, wounds Qin with a lance, but Luo Tong, a general under Qin, defeats Su. Wang Bochao, another enemy general, challenges Luo Tong, who wears very thick armor. Luo Tong underestimates his antagonist and is seriously injured in the abdomen because of carelessness. However, he keeps on fighting, finally slaying Wang Bochao before he himself succumbs.

Picture 58: *Overturning the Chariots*

The army of the Song Dynasty, led by Yue Fei, engages the Jin army in a fierce battle at Niutou (Bull Head) Hill. Defeated, the Jin troops flee, pursued by Gao Chong, a brave general under Yue Fei. To stop the Song troops, Jin Wuzhu, a royal prince and commander-in-chief of the Jin troops, orders armored vehicles to be released from a mountaintop. Powerful and fearless, Gao Chong overturns several of the vehicles with his spear. Finally, however, his battle horse fails him and he is crushed to death.

Feast of Peaches (Picture 60), *Havoc in Heaven* (Pictures 61 and 63), *Water Curtain Cave* (Picture 62), *Leopard Demon* (Picture 64) and *Havoc in the Dragon Palace* (Picture 65)

They are part of the repertoire of Peking Opera adapted from *Journey to the West*, a classical novel written in the 1770s. The major character in all these works is Sun Wukong the Monkey King. His legendary exploits include stealing peaches from the orchard of the Queen Mother and disturbing the planned feast for her birthday; causing an uproar in the Heavenly Palace because of discontent with the official rank the Jade Emperor has bestowed on him; proclaiming himself the Great Sage Equaling Heaven in the Water Curtain Cave on Flower and Fruit Mountain; and causing trouble in the Dragon Palace by demanding the gold-banded cudgel.

Picture 70: *The Women Generals of the Yang Family*

During the reign of Emperor Renzong (ruled 1023-1063) of the Song Dynasty, the army of Western Xia launches an attack on the northwestern border. Yang Zongbao, commander-in-chief of the Song troops, dies a heroic death in battle. The Song court is unable to find another competent commander to beat back the enemy. At this time, She Saihua, Yang Zongbao's grandmother, is already 100 years old. She takes up the post, and leads an army of women and her adolescent great-grandson Yang Wenguang against the enemy. The opera ends in victory for the Yang family women generals.

Picture 73: *Pavilion Overlooking the River*

An opera adapted from a poetic drama, which normally consists of four acts or song sequences, written by Guan Hanqing, the leading playwright of the Yuan Dynasty, it tells how the dandy son of an influential official schemes to take Tan Ji'er, the wife of Bai Shizhong, magistrate of Tanzhou, as his concubine. To achieve his aim, he contrives a scheme to frame Bai, and with the imperial edict and sword he goes to arrest the latter. Informed of the situation, Tan Ji'er disguises herself as a fisherman's wife and goes to meet the official's son at the Pavilion Overlooking the River. She gets him drunk and takes away the imperial edict, which she presents to the court as evidence of the plot. Confronted with the evidence, the villain has to plead guilty.

Picture 74: *Courtesan Su San on Her Way to Court*

This is an act from the long-established opera *Courtesan Yutangchun* (Yutangchun was the name used by Su San in the brothel), which was adapted from a Ming Dynasty novel titled *Yutangchun Meets Her Husband in a Lawsuit*, a love story about Su San and Wang Jinlong, son of the minister of rites.

After Wang Jinlong, Su San's lover, leaves to take the imperial examinations, Su San is sold to a merchant as a concubine. The merchant's wife poisons her husband to have an affair with another man, and blames the murder on Su San. She also bribes the Hongtong County magistrate, who sentences the courtesan to death. Meanwhile, Wang Jinlong passes the imperial examinations and is appointed to the post of official in charge of justice at Taiyuan, the capital of Shanxi Province. Reading the file on Su San, he has some misgivings about the murder case, and orders the courtesan to be brought to Taiyuan for another trial. This act depicts Su San on her way to the trial, reciting her grievances to Chong Gongdao, her escort. Overcome with sympathy, the old man takes her as his adopted daughter.

Acknowledgements

I would like to express my heartfelt thanks to the experts, artists and staff of the Beijing Opera Museum, the Beijing Fenglei Peking Opera Troupe and the Huguang Gild Hall for their assistance in the very difficult task of taking and collecting the photographs for this book and arranging them with the appropriate captions so that they provide the maximum convenience for readers to identify the different types of Peking Opera facial patterns.

Yu Dexiang

部分剧目剧情介绍

图13《群英会》

是一出百余年常演不衰的三国戏。公元208年，尚为东汉（25－220年）丞相的曹操率军进攻占据长江中游的吴国，吴国联合正在崛起的蜀国大败曹军于赤壁（传位于今湖北省蒲圻县境内）附近的江面上。群英会即取材于这一史实，表现赤壁之战前夕参战三方的将帅、谋士们运筹帷幄、奇谋巧计迭出的情节。

图14《甘露寺》

三国戏之一出。蜀国初兴时，曾借吴国的荆州屯兵。因其久借不还，吴主孙权与谋臣暗设计策：假托欲将孙权之妹孙尚香嫁与蜀主刘备，图谋将刘备拘为人质，索回荆州。谁知弄假成真，反成全了刘、孙的姻缘。甘露寺是一佛寺，传说刘备来吴后在此被孙权母相中，招赘为婿，所以用寺名作剧名。

此剧常与《回荆州》、《芦花荡》连演，合称《龙凤呈祥》（见图27、47）。后两出的情节为刘备成婚以后，久滞吴国不思返回荆州；随其来吴的赵云用诸葛亮预设的妙计，佯称曹操攻荆，催促刘备速返。孙尚香深明大义，背着母兄随刘备同行。

图15、26《空城计》

赤壁之战后的半个世纪中，魏、蜀、吴三国维持着均势状态，但是，魏、蜀之间仍时有交锋。公元228年蜀国伐魏，蜀丞相诸葛亮派大将马谡为先锋，因马谡刚愎自专，违背军令，致使战略要地街亭失守。司马懿引兵直奔兵力空虚的西城县。危急之中，诸葛亮设下空城计，他命将四面城门洞开，自己则装出气定神闲的样子坐在城楼上观景操琴；司马懿见状疑有重兵埋伏，反而不战而退。

《空城计》即指"城楼退兵"一节，前一部分剧名为《失街亭》（见图26），后为《斩马谡》。此三剧常常连演，俗称《失空斩》。

图16《打严嵩》

严嵩是十六世纪中叶明代的权臣，他当政期间操纵国事，侵吞军费，陷害朝臣，遭到正直之士的痛恨。一次，他命工匠秘造平天冠，图谋篡位，被御史邹应龙发觉，邹与开山王常宝童设计痛殴严嵩。

图17、38《华容道》

三国戏之一出。写赤壁之战后，曹操领十八骑兵败逃。行至华容道时，遭遇在此设伏截击的蜀将关羽。曹操动之以情衷求放行，关羽感念昔日兵败羁留曹营期间，曹操以礼相待之情，遂放他逃走。

图18《千里送京娘》

写宋太祖赵匡胤（公元960－976年在位）未登帝位时从盗窟中救出少女赵京娘，并护送她回家。途中，京娘对赵匡胤心生爱意，多次用言语试探，赵匡胤以为救人于危难，不应图报，遂婉言谢绝。

图19《秦香莲》

这是一出流传甚广的戏曲，其故事梗概为：北宋时，士人陈士美到京城汴梁（今河南开封）应科举考试，得中状元。为了攀附权贵，他竟隐瞒了已经娶妻生有一子一女的实情，做了皇室的驸马。三年后，他的妻子秦香莲携子女来寻，陈士美不仅不相认，还派人去杀母子三人，企图灭口。秦香莲遇救后向开封府包拯控告，包拯不顾众皇亲的阻挠，按律铡死陈士美。

图 20《法门寺》

明代掌管司礼监的宦官刘瑾（？－1510 年）权倾朝野，他抢掠民田，排斥异己，为所欲为。但是在这出戏里他却是秉公执法的正面人物。戏写他一次随侍皇太后到法门寺礼佛时，受理了一件因情而起的杀人冤案，他责令地方官对此案重新审理，结果真凶伏诛，受害的有情人终成眷属。

图 21、33、34《艳阳楼》

这是一出以武功见长的戏。戏中表演的许多武打功式是在别的戏中难得欣赏到的。剧情却颇简单，写北宋末年权相高俅的儿子高登将少女徐佩珠强掠至府中，安置在艳阳楼上。佩珠兄闻讯后，偕同其好友花逢春、秦仁、呼延豹夜入高宅，杀死高登，救出佩珠。

图 23《三打祝家庄》

祝家庄主朝奉和他的三个儿子一向仇视梁山义军，一次，时迁等人在投奔梁山途中留宿祝家父子开设的旅店，因时迁偷食了店中的鸡，被店伙扣留不放。此事激怒了梁山晁盖等将士，先后三次出兵攻打祝家庄，最后一次终于获胜。这出戏只演三次攻打祝家庄的激战情状和攻守双方的谋略。时迁等人投奔梁山至偷鸡被捉则属《时迁偷鸡》一剧（见图 75）的情节。

图 24、25、30《长坂坡》

三国戏之一出。一次，曹军南下至长江中游攻城掠地，刘备与众部将带着百姓转移。刘备的眷属在混乱中失散，部将赵云屡次冲入敌阵救出刘备的夫人与幼子阿斗。赵云怀抱阿斗，一次次冲过曹军的拦截，行至长坂坡时遇蜀将张飞挺身立马站在桥旁，他几声大喝，吓退了追兵，赵云终于脱险。

图 28《九江口》

13 世纪中期，中国处于元代之末，由于统治者的残暴和连年灾荒，反元的农民起义在全国蜂起。各起义军为了扩充势力，相互间时有争战。《九江口》一戏就取材于这段史实。剧情为义军首领陈友谅统兵攻打朱元璋（即后来的明太祖）领导的另一支义军，中途遭遇伏击，败逃至九江口，幸有元帅张定边化装成渔翁驾舟接应才脱险。而史实是公元 1363 年陈友谅在九江口中流矢身亡。

图 29、53、78《定军山》

是一出唱做念打并重的三国戏。演屡立战功的蜀国老将黄忠请缨攻打曹军重镇定军山，与曹军守将夏侯渊之战，初时难为胜负，后黄忠用计杀毙夏侯德、夏侯渊及其侄夏侯尚，夺取了定军山。

图 31、76《盗御马》

该剧又名《连环套》，取材于描写清代官吏施仕纶屡断怪案奇案的长篇小说《施公案》。

《盗御马》一剧写连环套寨主窦尔敦为报宿仇，假冒仇人之名盗取清帝赐予太尉邓九公的御马。案发后，施仕纶派智勇双全的部属黄天霸缉查。黄天霸在好友朱光祖的协助下勘破盗马案；窦尔敦感其不杀之恩，投案献马。

图 32《战宛城》

三国戏之一出。曹操攻宛城（在今河南省境内），宛城守将张绣不战而降。后因曹操掳占张绣的寡婶，张绣怒而夜袭曹营。骁将典韦为了护卫曹操力战而死，曹操仓惶而逃脱。

图 35《西门豹》

史书记载，战国（公元前 475－前 221 年）魏国邺地（今河北省临漳县邺镇）的三老、官吏和女巫假托为河伯娶妇以求免除水患，定期强选少女投入河中。西门豹任邺令后，决意破除这一迷信陋俗。到河伯娶妇时，他推说所选的女子不好，令女巫、三老去同河伯商量另选，把他们投入河中。从此，陋俗根绝，百姓称快。京剧《西门豹》即取材于这一历史故事。

图 36《将相和》

此剧取材于汉司马迁所著《史记·廉颇蔺相如列传》。《史记》是中国第一部纪传体通史，成书于公元前一世纪。

剧中的主人公廉颇、蔺相如是战国时期（公元前 475－前 221 年）赵国人，二人分别以文韬和武略有功于赵国，均被封为上卿，但蔺相如位居廉颇之上，廉颇居功自傲，不甘居蔺相如之下，扬言要寻机羞辱蔺相如；蔺相如不愿因将相不和而使外敌有隙可乘，一意忍让。廉颇得知后，深感悔疚，背负荆杖到相如府中请罪领责。从此，两人结为生死之交。

图 37《野猪林》

水浒戏之一出。北宋太尉高俅之子为了霸占禁军教头林冲的妻子，诬陷林冲持刀行刺太尉，论罪流放沧州，又买通解差在途中加害。林冲的好友僧人鲁智深，恐途中有失，暗中尾随，在野猪林救林冲脱险。继而，高俅及其子又派爪牙到沧州，欲置林冲于死地；林冲忍无可忍，杀死仇人，投奔梁山义军。

图 40《御果园》

此为《说唐》戏之一出。讲的是唐太宗李世民的两个哥哥指控李世民的部将尉迟恭假冒救驾之功。尉迟恭在隆冬时节服用了李靖之抗寒药后，于御果园当众重新演试，结果使得欲谋害李世民的黄壮当场毙命。

图 42《二进宫》

演绎明代一场宫廷权力之争的戏出。

公元 1572 年，明穆宗亡。因为太子年幼，由其嫡母李艳妃垂帘听政，李艳妃的父亲李良图谋篡位。定国公徐延昭和兵部侍郎杨波两次进宫向李艳妃陈言利害，终于使她辨明忠奸，请徐、杨二臣辅佐幼主，执掌国政。

图 43、55《草桥关》

演东汉光武帝（公元 25－57 年在位）时，草桥关守将姚期奉召回京供职。姚期之子姚刚打死帝妃之父郭荣，光武帝欲诛姚期全家。恰在此时，敌人来犯草桥关，接替姚期守关将领马武回朝请兵，光武帝遂命姚期父子戴罪出征。

图 44《霸王别姬》

这是一出凄婉壮烈的悲剧。写公元前 202 年西楚霸王项羽被汉王刘邦围困在垓下（今安徽省灵壁县以南），随征的宠姬虞姬为了使项羽突围时无所牵念，以剑自刎；项羽突围至乌江，悲愤交加，也自刎。

图45、46《穆柯寨》又名《降龙木》

此为《杨家将》故事之一。边关统帅杨延昭为破天门阵而命孟良、焦赞去穆柯寨求取降龙木。二人说话粗鲁而至双方见仗，孟、焦均败在寨主之女穆桂英手下。二人又请来杨延昭之子杨宗保助战，宗保又被穆桂英擒获。此剧又为之后的《穆桂英大破天门阵》做了很好的铺垫。

图48《除三害》

这出戏是传统剧目。讲得是晋朝宜兴人周处，酗酒好斗，横行一方，百姓们将他和猛虎、蛟蛟并称为"三害"。宜兴太守假扮老翁，以三害之说讽喻周处，说服其蒙生悔悟之心。于是周处打虎、斩蛟，改邪归正而三害皆除。

图49《李逵探母》

"水浒戏"之一。梁山义士李逵性情鲁莽而重孝义。此剧写李逵在回乡探母途中遇李鬼假冒他的名字拦路行劫，并谎称是为了奉养老母，出于无奈，李逵深信不疑，不仅没杀李鬼，反而解囊相赠。李逵回到家中，见母亲晚景凄凉，决定接到梁山奉养。不料归途中母被虎噬食，李逵怒而杀虎。

图51《金沙滩》

"杨家将"戏中之一出。写宋辽对峙时期，一次辽邀宋太宗（公元976－997年在位）到金沙滩赴会，杨继业料到其中有诈，让长子延平假扮太宗赴会，其余七子随行护卫。宴会进行中，辽国伏兵四起，延平用袖箭杀死辽主后被杀，二郎、三郎战死，四郎、八郎被擒，只有五郎、六郎、七郎冲出重围。

图52《八大锤》

公元1127年，北宋王朝被中国东北部女真族建立的金国所灭。同年，南宋王朝在临安（今浙江省杭州市）建立。南宋朝廷中正直的文臣武将力主抗击金兵，收复失地，名将岳飞（公元1103－1142年）率领的岳家军屡屡大败金兵。此剧即是表演岳家军中何元庆等四员战将各执双锤与金将陆文龙激战的情状。

图56《斩黄袍》

后周将领赵匡胤、郑恩（郑子明）、高怀德等于公元960年发动兵变，拥立赵匡胤为帝，改国号为宋。赵匡胤称帝后，韩龙献妹求荣，其妹韩素梅被封为妃，他也得宦进爵，并游街示荣，郑恩见后怒打韩龙。赵匡胤听信韩素梅的谗言，在醉中命斩郑恩，高怀德等苦谏不纳。郑恩的妻子陶三春闻讯，引兵围困宫城。赵匡胤酒醒后痛悔，央求高怀德调解；高怀德斩杀韩龙后，登城劝解陶三春。

图57《界牌关》

此剧取材于《薛仁贵征东》故事之一折。描写唐朝元帅薛仁贵部将罗通与敌将王伯超战于界牌关。王伯超战甲坚实，刀枪不入。而罗通却不慎被王刺伤腹部。罗忍痛盘肠大战，终于刺中王的咽喉而双双阵亡。剧情紧张激烈，颇具震憾力。

图58《挑滑车》

此剧以岳飞抗击金兵为题材。一次，岳家军与金兵鏖战牛头山，金兵大败。宋将高宠策马乘胜追击，金太祖之子兀术命金兵自山顶放滑车俯冲而下，以阻击宋军，高宠用枪连挑数辆，终因坐骑力尽而被滑车碾死。

图 60 《蟠桃会》、 图 61、63 《大闹天宫》、 图 62 《水帘洞》、 图 64 《金钱豹》、 图 65 《闹龙宫》
皆取材于16世纪70年代成书的中国神话小说《西游记》。各剧皆以神猴幻化的孙悟空为主角，分别扮演他偷食西王母桃园中的蟠桃，搅乱西王母的寿筵，因不满玉皇大帝的敕封，而大闹天宫，在花果山水帘洞自封齐天大圣，闯龙宫索要如意金箍棒作武器等等。

图 70 《杨门女将》
剧情为宋仁宗（公元1023 - 1063年在位）时，西夏国军队进犯宋西北边境，元帅杨宗保在抗击中阵亡。杨继业夫人、杨宗保祖母佘太君以百岁高龄毅然挂帅出征，杨家的女眷和其尚未成年的宗保之子杨文广都随其前往。全剧以杨门女将击溃西夏军，大获全胜而告终。

图 73 《望江亭》
根据13世纪剧作家关汉卿所作的杂剧改编，全名为《望江亭中秋切鲙旦》。
剧情为权贵杨衙内为了夺占白士中的妻子谭记儿，骗得皇帝的诏书和势剑来拿白士中。谭记儿得讯，扮作渔妇到望江亭见杨衙内，将他用酒灌醉，取得诏书和势剑，作为凭证与杨衙内对簿公堂，使其不得不服罪。

图 74 《女起解》
京剧传统剧目《玉堂春》中的一出。全剧取材于明代小说《玉堂春落难逢夫》，描写明代名妓苏三（即玉堂春）与吏部尚书之子王金龙的爱情故事。
《女起解》写苏三与王金龙离别以后，被诬杀人，囚禁在山西省洪洞县牢中，新任山西巡按到任，调审苏三杀人一案，苏三被押解赴太原受审。在赴太原途中，苏三苦诉不幸遭遇，解差崇公道深为同情，收她为义女。

82

鸣 谢

在与责编共商拟编本书之际，我们就有一个共识：采取以剧照为主，结合角色，分类简述的编法，增强阅读的趣味及爱好者对脸谱种类的识辨力。但这在相对时间内会给收集、拍摄和采写工作带来很大难度。不过在北京戏曲博物馆、北京风雷京剧团、湖广会馆戏楼等许多专家、艺术家及众多演职人员的鼎力协助和热情支持下，终于得以完成，在此谨致衷心的谢意！

对于篇目中涉及的艺术家表示敬意！

于得祥

目 录

Contents

图书在版编目(CIP)数据

京剧脸谱: 汉英对照 / 于得祥编绘 –北京: 外文出版社, 2000
ISBN 7-119-02486-8

Ⅰ.京… Ⅱ.于… Ⅲ. 京剧－脸谱－图集 Ⅳ.J821.5-64
中国版本图书 CIP 数据核字(1999)第 40559 号

Edited by: Yu Dexiang, Zhou Daguang
Photos by: Sun Shuming Wang Chunshu
       Lan Peijin Huo Jianying
       Zhao Dechun Yue Lianwei
Text by: Yu Dexiang, Liao Pin
Translator: Li Zhenguo
Editor: Zhou Daguang
Design: Zhou Daguang

编辑: 于得祥 周大光
摄影: 孙树明 王春树 兰佩瑾
     霍建赢 赵德春 岳连伟
撰稿: 于得祥 廖 频
翻译: 李振国
责任编辑: 周大光
设计: 周大光

京剧脸谱

于得祥 编撰

First Edition 2000

Peking Opera Facial Designs

ISBN 7-119-02486-8/J.1510

© Foreign Languages Press
Published by Foreign Languages Press
24 Baiwanzhuang Road, Beijing 100037, China
Home Page: http://www.flp.com.cn
E-mail Addresses: info@flp.com.cn
          sales@flp.com.cn
Printed in the People's Republic of China

© 外文出版社
外文出版社出版
(中国北京百万庄大街24号)
邮政编码 100037
外文出版社网址: http://www.flp.com.cn
外文出版社电子邮件地址: info@flp.com.cn
          sales@flp.com.cn
深圳麟德电脑设计制作有限公司电脑制版制作
天时印刷 (深圳) 有限公司印刷
版次 2000年6月第一版第一次印刷
(英汉)
书号 ISBN 7-119-02486-8/J.1510 (外)
004800 (精)